READ & RESPOND

Helping children discover the pleasure and pow~~er of reading~~

ONJALI Q. RAÚF

The Boy at the Back of the Class

FOR AGES 9–11

Published in the UK by Scholastic Education, 2021

Scholastic Distribution Centre, Bosworth Avenue, Tournament Fields, Warwick, CV34 6UQ

Scholastic Ireland, 89E Lagan Road, Dublin Industrial Estate, Glasnevin, Dublin, D11 HP5F

SCHOLASTIC and associated logos are trademarks and/or registered trademarks of Scholastic Inc.

www.scholastic.co.uk

© 2021 Scholastic

4 5 6 7 8 9   4 5 6 7 8 9 0 1 2 3
Printed and bound by Ashford Colour Press

This book is made of materials from well-managed, FSC®-certified forests and other controlled sources.

MIX
Paper | Supporting
responsible forestry
FSC® C011748

A CIP catalogue record for this book is available from the British Library.
ISBN 978-1407-18394-7

Extracts from *The National Curriculum in England, English Programme of Study* © Crown Copyright. Reproduced under the terms of the Open Government Licence (OGL). http://www.nationalarchives.gov.uk/doc/open-government-licence/version/3

Authors Eileen Jones
Editorial team Vicki Yates, Suzanne Adams, Julia Roberts, Rachel Morgan
Series designer Dipa Mistry
Typesetter QBS Learning
Illustrator Veronica Montoya / Advocate Art

Acknowledgements
The publishers gratefully acknowledge permission to reproduce the following material:
Orion Children's Books, an imprint of Hachette Children's Books, Carmelite House, 50 Victoria Embankment, London imprint, EC4Y 0DZ for the use of the text extracts, illustration and cover from *The Boy at the Back of the Class* written by Onjali Q. Raúf.
Every effort has been made to trace copyright holders for the works reproduced in this book, and the publishers apologise for any inadvertent omissions.

For supporting online resources go to:
www.scholastic.co.uk/read-and-respond/books/boy-at-the-back-of-the-class/online-resources
Access key: Refer

CONTENTS ▽

How to use Read & Respond in your classroom...

Read & Respond provides teaching ideas related to a specific well-loved children's book. Each Read & Respond book is divided into the following sections:

ABOUT THE BOOK AND AUTHOR

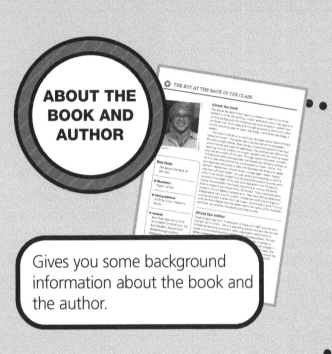

Gives you some background information about the book and the author.

GUIDED READING

Breaks the book down into sections and gives notes for using it, ideal for use with the whole class. A bookmark has been provided on page 12 containing **comprehension** questions. The children can be directed to refer to these as they read. Find comprehensive guided reading sessions on the supporting online resources.

SHARED READING

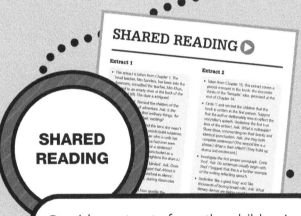

Provides extracts from the children's book with associated notes for focused work. There is also one non-fiction extract that relates to the children's book.

GRAMMAR, PUNCTUATION & SPELLING

Provides word-level work related to the children's book so you can teach grammar, punctuation, spelling and **vocabulary** in context.

PLOT, CHARACTER & SETTING

Contains activity ideas focused on the plot, characters and the setting of the story.

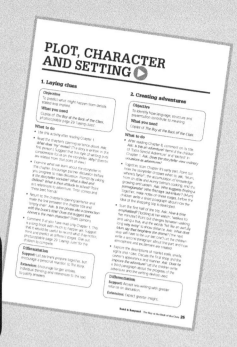

TALK ABOUT IT

Oracy, **fluency**, and speaking and listening activities. These activities may be based directly on the children's book or be broadly based on the themes and concepts of the story.

GET WRITING

Provides writing activities related to the children's book. These activities may be based directly on the children's book or be broadly based on the themes and concepts of the story.

ASSESSMENT

Contains short activities that will help you assess whether the children have understood concepts and curriculum objectives. They are designed to be informal activities to feed into your planning.

SUPPORTING ONLINE RESOURCE

Online you can find a host of supporting documents including planning information, comprehensive guided reading sessions and guidance on teaching reading.

www.scholastic.co.uk/read-and-respond/books/boy-at-the-back-of-the-class/online-resources
Access key: Refer

Help children develop a love of **reading for pleasure**.

Activities

The activities follow the same format:

- **Objective:** the objective for the lesson. It will be based upon a curriculum objective, but will often be more specific to the focus being covered.

- **What you need:** a list of resources you need to teach the lesson, including photocopiable pages.

- **What to do:** the activity notes.

- **Differentiation:** this is provided where specific and useful differentiation advice can be given to support and/or extend the learning in the activity. Differentiation by providing additional adult support has not been included as this will be at a teacher's discretion based upon specific children's needs and ability, as well as the availability of support.

The activities are numbered for reference within each section and should move through the text sequentially – so you can use the lesson while you are reading the book. Once you have read the book, most of the activities can be used in any order you wish.

Section	Activity	Curriculum objectives
Guided reading		Comprehension: To predict what might happen from details stated and implied.
Shared reading	1	Comprehension: To draw inferences such as inferring characters' feelings, thoughts and motives from their actions, and to justify inferences with evidence.
	2	Comprehension: To discuss and evaluate how writers use language, including figurative language, considering the impact on the reader.
	3	Comprehension: To predict what might happen from details stated and implied.
	4	Comprehension: To identify how language, structure and presentation contribute to meaning.
Grammar, punctuation and spelling	1	Vocabulary, grammar and punctuation: To know how words are related by meaning as synonyms and antonyms. (Appendix 2)
	2	Vocabulary, grammar and punctuation: To use modal verbs or adverbs to indicate degrees of possibility.
	3	Word reading: To pronounce words containing the letter string 'ough'. (Appendix 1)
	4	Vocabulary, grammar and punctuation: To recognise vocabulary and structures that are appropriate for formal speech and writing.
	5	Vocabulary, grammar and punctuation: To use and understand grammatical terminology accurately and appropriately.
	6	Vocabulary, grammar and punctuation: To understand that 'cial' is common after a vowel letter and 'tial' after a consonant letter, but there are some exceptions.
Plot, character and setting	1	Comprehension: To predict what might happen from details stated and implied.
	2	Comprehension: To identify how language, structure and presentation contribute to meaning.
	3	Comprehension: To make comparisons within and across books.
	4	Comprehension: To infer characters' feelings, thoughts and motives from their actions.
	5	Comprehension: To discuss and evaluate how authors use language, including figurative language, considering the impact on the reader.
	6	Comprehension: To identify how language, structure and presentation contribute to meaning.
	7	Comprehension: To identify and discuss themes and conventions in and across a wide range of writing.
	8	Comprehension: To provide reasoned justifications for their views.

Section	Activity	Curriculum objectives
Talk about it	1	Spoken language: To participate in discussions, role play and improvisations.
	2	Spoken language: To give well-structured narratives for different purposes, including for expressing feelings.
	3	Spoken language: To consider and evaluate different viewpoints.
	4	Spoken language: To articulate and justify answers, arguments and opinions. Comprehension: To infer characters' feelings, thoughts and motives.
	5	Spoken language: To ask relevant questions to extend their understanding and knowledge.
	6	Spoken language: To select and use appropriate registers for effective communication.
Get writing	1	Composition: To use a wide range of devices to build cohesion within and across paragraphs.
	2	Composition: To identify the audience for and purpose of the writing, selecting the appropriate form and using other similar writing as models for their own.
	3	Composition: To evaluate by assessing the effectiveness of others' writing.
	4	Composition: To write in narrative form, by describing settings, characters and atmosphere.
	5	Composition: To plan their writing by noting and developing initial ideas, drawing on reading.
	6	Composition: To draft and write by selecting appropriate grammar and vocabulary, understanding how such choices can change and enhance meaning.
Assessment	1	Comprehension: To provide reasoned justification for their views.
	2	Comprehension: To explain and discuss their understanding of what they have read.
	3	Composition: To write a narrative, describing settings, characters and atmosphere and integrating dialogue to convey character and advance the action.
	4	Comprehension: To infer characters' feelings, thoughts and motives from their actions, and to justify inferences with evidence.
	5	Composition: To note and develop initial ideas, drawing on reading and research where necessary.
	6	Composition: To select the appropriate form and use other similar writing as models for their own.

Key facts

The Boy at the Back of the Class

◉ **Illustrator:**
Pippa Curnick

◉ **First published:**
2018 by Orion Children's Books

◉ **Awards:**
Blue Peter Best Story 2019
Nominated for Books Are My Bag Readers' Award 2019 (Breakthrough Author)
Waterstones Children's Book Prize 2019

About the book

The Boy at the Back of the Class is a children's novel for our times. Written in 2018, this exciting, London adventure story is set against a sombre background: the contemporary issue of asylum seekers from the Syrian war. Informative and thought-provoking, the book is ideal for the maturing tastes of upper Key Stage 2 and lower Key Stage 3 readers.

The story is told by an anonymous nine-year-old at Nelson Primary School in London. The reader learns quickly about the storyteller's life with a single mother, little money, a close-knit band of three loyal school friends and a zest for adventure. The spotlight also falls on the new boy, Ahmet, a silent non-English speaker who sits looking scared and sad at the back of the class. Through welcoming winks and gifts, including an exotic pomegranate, the friends win Ahmet's confidence, his first real smile and the first word spoken to them: 'home'. The pomegranate also causes a fight with Brendan-the-Bully and reveals Ahmet's fearlessness. Ahmet shows courage again when, having acquired sufficient English, he uses speech and drawings to tell the story of his family's escape from Syria and the perilous journey which resulted in the death of his sister and separation from his parents. Led by the storyteller, the friends determine to reunite the family before migrants are refused entry into Britain. They make bold plans, revisions and emergency replacements. They have daring adventures, independent trips around London, involvement with the emergency services and even a letter from the Queen. Do the plans work? It is not until the final chapter that the reader learns the name of the storyteller and finds out whether the adventure brings success.

About the author

Onjali Q Raúf was born in Newcastle in England in 1981 and she was brought up in London. She is a bestselling author and also the founder of Making Herstory, a women's rights organisation which aims to create a more equal world for women and girls everywhere. She also delivers emergency aid and parcels to refugee families in camps in Calais and Dunkirk. It was her experience of meeting Syrian people in a Calais refugee camp that inspired her to write her debut novel, *The Boy at the Back of the Class*. Raúf was named by the BBC as one of the 100 inspiring and influential women from around the world (2019).

GUIDED READING ▶

Chapters 1 to 3

Identify these personal pronouns and adjectives in the early paragraphs: 'I', 'me', 'my'. Ask: *Is the writing in the first or third person?* (First) *What advantage is there?* (The storyteller is within the action.) Discuss question 2 on the bookmark together. Point out: stationery, Tintin adventures, London, dislike of maths, friendliness, sympathy (but no name). Discuss question 1 on the bookmark.

Point out Chapter 2's title and read aloud the second paragraph. Suggest that the detailed description of his eyes emphasises the focus on Ahmet. Ask: *What rumours does Jennie spread about Ahmet?* (that he had done something bad in his old school and was dangerous) *Do the four friends believe this?* Invite discussion of question 4 on the bookmark. Comment that Mrs Khan's smile and wink are pleasing reminders of Dad.

Comment on the storyteller's determined, friendly winking in Chapter 3. Ask: *What shows protectiveness?* (The storyteller's concern about Brendan's possible behaviour.) *What suggests that Mr Thompson does not disapprove of Brendan's bullying?* ('Rascal' is a gentle word and winking is friendly.) Agree that 'seclusion' means being kept separate. Let the children use question 1 on the bookmark to discuss the likely reason for Ahmet's seclusion.

Chapters 4 to 7

Investigate the friends' conversation about Ahmet, using question 4 on the bookmark. Ask: *What do they learn from the adults' conversation?* (Ahmet is a refugee.) Invite discussion on question 5 on the bookmark. Explore the two adults' contrasting attitudes by using question 6. Emphasise the storyteller's determined offer of friendship. *What promises that Ahmet will soon give a return smile of friendship?* (He looks and nods.)

After reading Chapter 5, use question 2 on the bookmark and share information learned since the end of Chapter 1: age; mum's job; father dead;

little money; Uncle Lenny's family. Consider Mum's reaction to 'refugee kid' and explore her patient explanation of refugee hardship. Point out 'bullies'. Ask: *Does a simple word help the storyteller to understand?* Relate question 7 on the bookmark to the storyteller's descriptions of meals from Mrs Abbey and the question list.

Read Chapter 6 and use question 3 on the bookmark to investigate the friends' discussion on refugees. Point out willingness to listen to one another; sympathy for war victims; awareness of parental views. Comment on the significance of 'his lion eyes looked happy' and the spoken 'friends' as Ahmet relaxes. Consider the information about Syria, the mysterious lady in the scarf, and Brendan's dangerous 'scowl'.

In Chapter 7, contrast the happy football game with the nervous confusion caused by Brendan. Identify Brendan's manipulative 'sad' expression on seeing Mr Irons. Ask: *Does Mr Irons respond reasonably? What do the other adults think?* Use question 6 on the bookmark for group discussion. Suggest that the children use questions 5 and 7 on the bookmark as they consider the chapter title.

Chapters 8 to 10

Link Chapter 8's title to the book's second paragraph and theme of 'adventures'. Connect the storyteller's questions in Chapter 5 with the present conversation with Mum. Ask: *Why does the storyteller ask about favourite Syrian fruits?* (Ahmet needs a healthy treat.) Explore Mum's ability to create games: the 'pomegranate' spelling and the shopping trip 'adventure'. Invite discussion of question 8 on the bookmark.

After reading Chapter 9, re-read the description of the pomegranate and discuss question 7 on the bookmark together. Ask: *How does Ahmet show surprised delight?* (He mentions 'home' and gives a proper smile.) *Why does the storyteller feel brave and big enough to confront Brendan? Why is Ahmet so angry? How do other children react afterwards?*

(Ahmet becomes popular.) Use question 11 on the bookmark for group discussion.

Discuss question 1 on the bookmark, focusing on predicting Chapter 10's contents. Investigate Brendan's spiteful acts (smashed pot; worms; damaged bag).

Explore Ahmet's story. Ask: *Why do the children feel 'strange' afterwards?* (It is true.) *What does the storyteller understand?* (Ahmet is brave.) *What does the storyteller now understand about Ahmet's bag?* (It has come with him.) Discuss question 11 on the bookmark.

Chapters 11 to 13

Compare the storyteller's new questions in Chapter 11 with the original list. Ask: *How are these different?* (They involve specific detail about people and places.) Contrast Lenny and Christina's attitudes to information about Ahmet, using question 6 on the bookmark. Point out the news that Grandma Jo helped refugees. Ask*: Why can the storyteller not focus on Scrabble?* (The storyteller feels so proud of Grandma Jo.)

Point out Brendan's insults in Chapter 12. Ask: *What is Ahmet's reaction?* (He is ready to fight.) Consider what Ahmet and the storyteller share (enjoyment of Tintin; they miss their fathers). Ask: *Where is Ahmet's father?* (Ahmet does not know.) Point out Ahmet's willingness to confide in his sympathetic friend. Let the children explore the two characters' conversation and discuss question 8 on the bookmark.

After reading Chapter 13, identify the important detail of the overheard conversation: 'the borders will be closed by the end of the month'. Investigate Josie, Michael and the storyteller's library meeting. Ask: *Why is Tom not involved?* (He is in the playground with Ahmet.) *What do the four friends decide later?* (They must reunite Ahmet and his parents.)

Chapters 14 to 17

Discuss question 3 on the bookmark after reading Chapter 14. Emphasise the friends' mutual kindness, as Josie reassures the storyteller. Ask: *Who is downhearted?* (The storyteller has no plan.) Emphasise the respectful consideration given to each plan. Ask: *Which plan excites them most?* (Michael's) *What spoils it?* (The letter will not be read in time.) *What makes the chapter end hopeful?* (The storyteller's plan will be 'fantastic'.) Suggest the children discuss question 8 on the bookmark.

Read Chapter 15 and ask: *Who is the girl in the nightmare probably based on?* (Syrah) *Who else is in the nightmare?* (Dad) Point out that the storyteller's thoughts often turn to Dad. Ask: *What prompts the Greatest Idea in the World?* (the picture in a Tintin comic) Examine the idea and point out the storyteller's excitement. Use question 12 on the bookmark for discussion.

After reading Chapter 16, identify enthusiasm for the storyteller's idea and childish certainty that the Queen will receive the letter. Point out Michael's careless tripping, reinforcing the point in Chapter 2 of 'bumping into things'. Explore the whispered planning, secrecy and deceit. Ask: *Is the storyteller right to reveal Ahmet's secret to the Queen?* Examine the letter's language and use question 7 on the bookmark for discussion.

Read the next chapter together and ask: *Why does Michael bump into a lamp post?* (He is excited.) *Why are the friends disappointed by Ms Hemsi and Ahmet?* (They seem normal.) *When does worry replace excitement?* (Tuesday) Use question 3 on the bookmark for class discussion of the Emergency Plan. Ask: *Do they decide fairly who should carry out the plan?* Let the children discuss question 8 on the bookmark in groups.

Chapters 18 to 20

Read Chapter 18 and point out the storyteller's tendency to relate to Tintin adventures. Ask: *Why do they say they look 'puffy like a blowfish'?* (Their clothes are under their school uniform.) Discuss question 7 on the bookmark to investigate the Queen's presents. Point out how the friends check their arrangements. Ask: *What problems occur at the Tube station?* (crowds and the ticket machine) *How much does Stan charge?* (nothing)

After reading Chapter 19, ask: *What surprises the storyteller about the palace?* (the crowds) *Why does the storyteller, holding out the note, not call to the guards inside the gate?* (The storyteller's voice seems 'stuck'.) Investigate the actions from 'I began to move' (feeling of running underwater; clambering over barriers; running onto the road; approaching a guard; calling out; collapsing). Let the children discuss question 9 on the bookmark.

Read the next chapter together and ask: *What emphasises the seriousness of what has happened?* (Tom cries.) Comment on 'gently' when the Queen's Special Guard speaks to the storyteller and his smile when he reads the note. Suggest the children use question 7 on the bookmark as they share ideas. Ask: *Does Davinder find something funny? Is the exciting trip home really enjoyable?* (No, school and parents will be angry.)

Chapters 21 to 23

After reading Chapter 21, investigate Mum and the neighbours' reaction to the incident. Discuss questions 7 and 8 on the bookmark together, as you consider dialogue and actions. Ask: *Why does Mum shout and hug? Are neighbours friendlier? Is Mum braver with Mr Greggs?*

Emphasise Mum's important explanation about difference. Ask: *Does the storyteller now understand people's fear of difference? What angers, then amuses Mum about Stan's interview?* (Stan ridicules the question.) Point out the storyteller's optimism and hope of more adventures.

Read the next chapter together and discuss how parents and teachers collaborate to protect the friends from the media. Ask: *How does Mr Irons*

let the children down? (He lets the press surround them.) Explore the events in Mrs Sanders' office. Ask: *Why does Ahmet stand next to the storyteller? What does he feel? Why is the newspaper headline hopeful?* (Readers may support Ahmet.) Discuss question 6 on the bookmark together.

Point out the reference to Dad in Chapter 23: 'someone you love most in the world dies'. Comment that Mr Irons hears Brendan's song, but ignores it. Read the description of the fight and Ahmet's ferocity. *What shows later that Ahmet is no longer afraid?* (Ahmet looked at Brendan and grinned.) *What probably happens to Mr Irons?* Let the children discuss question 11 on the bookmark.

Chapter 24 to the end

Comment on the friends, and Ahmet's increasing concern in Chapter 24. Ask: *What has given Ahmet jumping and climbing practice?* (fences) Investigate Mum's anger at Mr Fry's lies. Ask: *What is Mum's plan?* (The children are interviewed.) Emphasise interest in Grandma Jo. Ask: *How effective is the newspaper report? How do Josie's parents change?* (They no longer fear someone new.) Use question 10 on the bookmark for discussion.

After reading Chapter 25, consider the children's fame and adults' increased friendliness. Ask: *Why are the four friends called to Mrs Sanders' office? What have the Guards brought?* (a letter from the Queen) Investigate the content of the letter. Ask: *Does it sound hopeful?* (Yes, many people are trying to find Ahmet's parents.) Let the children discuss question 10 on the bookmark.

Read the final chapter and explore people's changed behaviour and the Queen's invitation. Ask: *Who leaves Dad's card out? Is this thoughtful?* Agree that the storyteller, although sad, wants to remember him. Ask: *What is Ahmet taking to the Palace?* (his rucksack) Point out 'panicked' and his explanation. Ask: *What name is revealed?* (Alexa is the storyteller.) *What are Ahmet's special words?* ('best friend') *What does the document grant?* (Ahmet and his family can stay.) Discuss question 12 on the bookmark.

The Boy at the Back of the Class
By Onjali Q Raúf

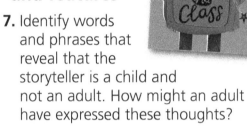

Focus on...
Meaning

1. What predictions can you make now about the main focus of the story? How much do the book's cover, title and this chapter help you?

2. What do you know about the child who is telling the story? What surprising piece of information has been omitted?

3. How do the four friends treat one another? Do they show respect for one another's ideas and feelings? Support your opinion with evidence from the text.

4. Why do the four friends welcome Ahmet into their group? What is their attitude towards him?

Focus on...
Organisation

5. How is the book organised? Is this an effective structure? How helpful are the chapter titles in guiding the reader?

6. What devices does the author use to build characters and to distinguish between their attitudes and viewpoints?

The Boy at the Back of the Class
By Onjali Q Raúf

Focus on...
Language and features

7. Identify words and phrases that reveal that the storyteller is a child and not an adult. How might an adult have expressed these thoughts?

8. Is dialogue used effectively? Does it reveal information about characters? Give two examples and explain what it told you.

Focus on...
Purpose, viewpoints and effects

9. What is the purpose of this chapter? How is the author creating excitement?

10. What effect does Mum's plan have on some adult characters? How do they change their attitude to Ahmet? Why are they no longer afraid of newcomers?

11. How does the author want you to regard Ahmet? Does she try to make you pity him or to admire his courage?

12. Do you think that this book is just an adventure story or does it have a deeper meaning?

SHARED READING ▶

Extract 1

- This extract is taken from Chapter 1. The head teacher, Mrs Sanders, has been into the classroom, consulted the teacher, Mrs Khan, pointed to an empty chair at the back of the room and left. The class is intrigued.

- Circle 'exciting'. Remind the children of the storyteller's love of adventure. Ask: *Is the storyteller ready to find ordinary things, for example an empty chair, exciting?*

- Underline the clause 'and this time she wasn't alone'. Suggest that the words build suspense; the reader waits to discover who is with her. Underline 'A boy none of us had ever seen before.' Ask: *Is it a phrase or a sentence?* Explain that the phrase is punctuated as a short sentence. *Why?* (It heightens the drama.)

- Underline 'eyes that hardly blinked'. Ask: *Does the lack of movement suggest that Ahmet is relaxed?* (no) Underline 'watched in silence', contrasting the confident, staring classmates and the tense stranger.

- Circle 'sorry'. Point out how quickly the storyteller shows sympathy. Underline the long first sentence of the penultimate paragraph. Ask: *What difficulties does the storyteller identify?* Circle 'new to a place' and 'people you don't know'. Ask: *Are these likely problems for anyone in Ahmet's situation?*

- Underline 'I would be friends with the new boy'. Comment on the speed of the decision. Ask: *What does this suggest about the storyteller's character?*

- Circle 'scared' and 'sad', the first definite picture of Ahmet. Underline 'at the back of our class'. Ask: *Could being placed at the back of the class affect Ahmet's feelings? Why?*

Extract 2

- Taken from Chapter 15, this extract covers a pivotal moment in the book: the storyteller thinks of the 'fantastic' idea, promised at the end of Chapter 14.

- Circle 'I' and remind the children that this book is written in the first person. Suggest that the author deliberately tries to reflect the storyteller's speech. Underline the first two lines of the extract. Ask: *What is noticeable?* Share ideas, commenting on their brevity and identical punctuation. Ask: *Are they both complete sentences?* (The second line is a phrase.) *What is their effect?* (They build up drama and excitement.)

- Investigate the first proper paragraph. Circle 'And'. Ask: *Do sentences usually begin with 'And'?* Suggest that this is a further example of the writing reflecting speech.

- Underline 'like a giant frog' and 'like thousands of boring bread rolls'. Ask: *What literary devices are being used?* (similes) *What are the comparisons between? Are they effective?* Explore how the first simile presents a picture of fast, sudden movement as the brain makes unlikely connections; the second one is slow and predictable.

- Examine the pictorial diagram. Ask: *Why is this included? How does it help the storyteller?* (The diagram will make the plan easier to explain and remember.) Circle 'greatest surprise'. Share ideas on what this could be. Ask: *Will it be a complete success?*

- Underline 'I stared at it and went over it again and again'. Ask: *Why does the storyteller do this?* (The storyteller is determined the plan must work.)

- Circle 'secret'. Ask: *Why is this essential?*

Extract 3

- This extract is from Chapter 26 and is part of the story's climax. Ms Duncan, from the Home Office, other adults and all the children are in the classroom.

- Circle 'deathly silent'. Ask: *Do the children recognise the seriousness of the occasion?*

- Underline 'like someone was playing drums inside my tummy'. Ask: *What literary device is this?* (a simile) *Why is the comparison effective?* (It describes a mental mood producing a physical reaction.)

- Circle 'special news'. Ask: *Does the reader know the news?* (no) Circle 'share' and emphasise its importance. Ask: *What does 'share' show Ahmet?* (He feels part of the class.) Remind the children of his withdrawn lack of eye contact in Chapter 1.

- Underline 'plain white envelope'. Investigate Ahmet's reaction to it. Ask: *What shows Mrs Hemsi's emotional state?* Underline 'laughing and crying all at once'.

- Underline 'best friend'. Ask: *Why is it important?* Refer to the storyteller's silent promise in Chapter 1 to 'be friends with the new boy'.

- Circle 'Alexa'. Ask: *Who is she?* (the storyteller) *Why is the name important here?* (She has been unnamed so far.) Discuss why the author has left her unnamed. Ask: *Does it allow both boys and girls to identify with the storyteller?*

- Underline 'Happy birthday'. Remind the children that birthdays are not usually celebrated much by Alexa. Discuss why, referring to the beginning of Chapter 26.

- Examine the final paragraph. Underline 'Ahmet's eyes looked so big', and circle 'nervous' and 'shake'. Ask: *Are they connected? What makes Alexa clumsy?*

Extract 4

- This extract, a non-fiction text, provides information about Syrian pomegranate trees.

- Underline and read aloud the opening paragraph. Ask: *What does it achieve?* (It introduces the topic.) *What background detail does the paragraph supply?* (It explains the name.)

- Question the children about divisions in the remaining text (paragraphs) Underline the bold words before paragraphs two to five. Ask: *What are they? What is their purpose?* (Explain that such subheadings are common in information text. They help the reader to access information.)

- Circle '5 to 10m', '200 years', and 'Middle East'. Emphasise that they identify size, age and location. Explain that such facts are essential in a text giving botanical and geographical information.

- Circle 'citrus' in the fourth paragraph. Explain that the word describes a particular classification of tree. The correct term gives technical authenticity to the text.

- Highlight and identify a bullet point. Ask: *Why are these marks useful?* Agree that the organisational device divides the list into manageable parts.

- Read paragraph four aloud. Refer to Chapter 9 of the novel and the storyteller's description and Mum's instructions on eating a pomegranate. Ask: *Is the fiction realistic? Does it match the facts?*

- Underline 'is surrounded' in the fourth paragraph and 'is held' in the final paragraph. Identify each as a passive verb: a verb in which the person or thing receiving the action is the subject of the sentence. Circle and identify 'seed' as the subject of the first passive verb, and 'festival' as the subject of the last.

Extract 1

It was all very serious and exciting. But before we could start guessing about what was going on, Mrs Sanders came back, and this time she wasn't alone.

Standing behind her was a boy. A boy none of us had ever seen before. He had short dark hair and large eyes that hardly blinked and smooth pale skin.

'Everyone,' said Mrs Khan, as the boy went and stood next to her. 'This is Ahmet, and he'll be joining our class from today. He's just moved to London and is new to the school, so I hope you'll all do your very best to make him feel welcome.'

We all watched in silence as Mrs Sanders led him to the empty chair. I felt sorry for him because I knew he wouldn't like sitting next to Clarissa very much. She still missed Dena, and everyone knew she hated boys – she says they're stupid and smell.

I think it must be one of the worst things in the world to be new to a place and have to sit with people you don't know. Especially people that stare and scowl at you like Clarissa was doing. I made a secret promise to myself right there and then that I would be friends with the new boy. I happened to have some lemon sherbets in my bag that morning and I thought I would try and give him one at break-time. And I would ask Josie and Tom and Michael if they would be his friends too.

After all, having four new friends would be much better than having none. Especially for a boy who looked as scared and as sad as the one now sitting at the back of our class.

Extract 2

I had it!

An idea!

And it was without a doubt, quite possibly, the Greatest Idea in the World! It leapt right into my head, just like a giant frog, and jumped around until I knew it had to work! It just had to!

You can always tell when you've had a Greatest Idea in the World because it pops up from nowhere. Ordinary ideas take an awfully long time to become an idea because they're ordinary, so your brain can't get excited about them and has to make them slowly – like thousands of boring bread rolls being baked in an extra slow oven. But when an idea is truly great, it doesn't take any time at all – it just suddenly appears and makes your eyes go wide and your brain feel as if it's just been pushed out of bed.

Jumping to my feet, I got out my exercise book and drew out my plan. This is what the Greatest Idea in the World looked like:

When I had finished, I stared at it and went over it again and again in my head. I knew right away that it would work – but only if Tom and Josie and Michael helped and kept it all a secret.

Extract 3

Everyone was deathly silent now, and I could feel my whole chest beating so hard that it felt like someone was playing drums inside my tummy.

Ms Duncan carried on. 'Today, I had the pleasure of bringing Ahmet some special news. And he has very kindly said that he would like to share it with all of you. Ahmet?'

She held out a plain white envelope that had no address on it, and offered it to him.

But Ahmet didn't take it, and whispered something to Ms Hemsi instead.

Ms Hemsi frowned at first, but then laughing and crying all at once, gestured at me to come up. 'He would like his best friend to read it to everyone,' she explained.

For a moment, I couldn't move. Then Josie gave me a kick under the table that made me stand up and slowly walk over to where Ahmet was standing.

Ms Duncan waited until I was standing in front of her and, holding out the envelope to me, said, 'A very happy birthday, Alexa, from all of us. Thanks to you – and to Josie and Michael and Tom of course – there have been thousands of people writing in and signing petitions and calling our offices, just to ask how they could help Ahmet and lots of other refugee children like him. And because of that…well…here you go…'

Ahmet nodded and added, 'Happy birthday, best friend.'

I opened my mouth, but I think all my words must have disappeared and my brain had stopped working, because I couldn't really think any thoughts any more.

Ahmet tapped the envelope in my hand, and said, 'You read it! For me…'

I tried to take the piece of paper out of the envelope, but there were so many eyes staring at me and Ahmet's eyes looked so big that my fingers got nervous and started to shake.

Extract 4

The Syrian Pomegranate

The name 'pomegranate' has its sources in two old languages: Latin and French. The Latin words were *pomum* (apple) and *granatum* (seeded). The old French name was *pomme-grenade*.

What is a pomegranate tree?

The pomegranate tree is a fruit-bearing shrub or small tree, that can grow to a height of 5 to 10m. It originated in Syria and countries nearby. Today it is cultivated widely throughout the Middle East, the Mediterranean, regions of Africa and Asia, and it is even grown successfully in Arizona and California. Some specimens are very long lived, and there are trees in France that are thought to be over 200 years old.

How can you recognise the tree?

The pomegranate tree has multiple spiny branches, narrow, glossy leaves and distinctive bright red flowers. These magnificent trumpet-shaped flowers are valued for their beauty.

What is the pomegranate fruit like?

The pomegranate fruit is usually red-purple in colour. It is an unusual fruit – neither a citrus fruit, like an orange, nor a stone fruit, like a plum. On the outside, it does indeed resemble an apple, as its Latin and French language roots suggest. However, its physical structure is very different in many ways:

- The pomegranate varies in size between a lemon and a grapefruit.
- There are two parts: an outer, hard pericarp and an inner, spongy mesocarp.
- The mesocarp contains tiny, edible seeds.
- Each seed is surrounded by a deep pink or red jewel-like capsule of juicy flesh.
- The number of seeds can vary from 200 to 1400.

Where is it celebrated?

The town of Darkush in Syria is famous for its pomegranate trees. An annual festival is held in October each year to celebrate that year's crop of pomegranates.

GRAMMAR, PUNCTUATION AND SPELLING ▶

1. Word relations

Objective
To know how words are related by meaning as synonyms and antonyms.

What you need
Copies of *The Boy at the Back of the Class*.

What to do
- Use this activity after reading Chapter 1.

- Ask: *What is a synonym? What is an antonym?* Explain that two words are synonyms when they have the same or similar meanings; they are antonyms when they have opposite meanings.

- Let the children use individual whiteboards to write a synonym and an antonym for 'big'. Ask them to hold up their boards and compare results. Confirm that answers may vary. Write 'big, large, little' on the board.

- Refer the children to the second paragraph of Chapter 1 and the adjective 'huge'. Let the children write a synonym and an antonym. Compare answers before writing 'huge, enormous, tiny' on the board. Ask: *How does the second set of words differ from the first set?* (The words are more extreme.)

- Ask the children to search the first three paragraphs in Chapter 1 for twelve different adjectives. Share answers, confirming whether or not a word is an adjective. Write this list: 'empty', 'special', 'exciting', 'best', 'new', 'jumpy', 'nice', 'boring', 'tall', 'long', 'favourite', 'important'.

- The children should write the headings 'adjective', 'synonym' and 'antonym' in a row and then copy your list in the adjective column. Remind them that a dictionary or a thesaurus can help them.

Differentiation
Support: Reduce the list and encourage partner discussion.

Extension: Ask children to work on adjectives in the next three paragraphs.

2. Degrees of possibility

Objective
To use modal verbs or adverbs to indicate degrees of possibility.

What you need
Copies of *The Boy at the Back of the Class*, photocopiable page 22 'Degrees of possibility'.

What to do
- Complete this activity after reading Chapter 4.

- Define 'degree of possibility' as the likelihood of an event occurring. This can be suggested by an adverb, for example, 'Mum and I are definitely going by bus'.

- Refer the children to the first paragraph of Chapter 3 and point out 'probably'. Indicate 'Maybe' in the early dialogue of Chapter 4. Identify them both as adverbs of possibility. Ask: *Which adverb makes the possibility sound stronger?* (probably) Confirm that some adverbs may show less certainty than others.

- Explain that possibility may also be indicated by a modal verb. Remind the children that this is a helping verb, used to support the main verb. Identify these examples in Chapter 1: 'could', 'wouldn't', ''ll' (will), 'would'.

- Write these two sentences on the board: 'Michael could fall off his chair.'; 'I must take my money with me.' Ask: *Which modal verb sounds definite?* (must) *Which only sounds possible?* (could)

- Give out photocopiable page 22 'Degrees of possibility'. Explain that they must sort the adverbs into two groups before adding them to the sentences. In the second part they must identify the modal verbs and assess their possibility.

Differentiation
Support: Let children work in pairs to decide on possibility.

Extension: Ask children to use the modal verbs in sentences.

3. Letter-strings

Objective
To pronounce words containing the letter-string 'ough'.

What you need
Copies of *The Boy at the Back of the Class*.

What to do

- Use this activity after reading Chapter 22.

- Refer the children to Chapter 22, when the friends are sent to speak to the police in Mrs Sanders' office. The storyteller talks of being scared about 'something you never, ever thought would happen'. Write the quotation on the board for the children to read aloud.

- Underline 'thought', circling the 'ough' letter string. Explain that is one of the trickiest spellings in English. Ask: *Can you suggest why?* (It changes its pronunciation frequently.)

- Write 'ought', 'through', 'cough', and 'tough' on the board. Let the children say them to a partner. Ask: *Does the sound made by the letter-string 'ough' stay the same?* Agree that it differs in each word. Demonstrate this by saying each word separately, and the children writing a rhyming word for each. Compare the results.

- Write these on the board: 'borough', 'dough', 'bough', 'cough', 'although', 'trough', 'plough', 'thorough'. Ask the children to write them in pairs of words where the letters 'ough' make the same sound. Encourage the children to check by saying the words aloud to themselves, before they use six of the words in written sentences.

Differentiation
Support: Encourage oral partner work and reduce the number of sentences asked for.

Extension: Ask children to write sentences using these words: 'rough', 'enough', 'ought'. Can they think of a rhyming partner for each?

4. Formal or informal?

Objective
To recognise appropriate forms and vocabulary for formal speech and writing.

What you need
Copies of *The Boy at the Back of the Class*, photocopiable page 23 'Formal or informal?'

What to do

- Work on this activity after completing the book.

- Direct the children to the letter from the Home Office in Chapter 26. Ask: *Is it a formal or informal piece of writing?* (formal) *How can you tell?* Share ideas, investigating the language used.

- Point out the difficult, formal vocabulary used: 'status', 'located', 'deceased', 'granted permanent asylum', 'reunification', 'imminent'. Point out Alexa's confusion about the document and suggest that some of the words would confuse any reader. Ask: *Why are they used?* Point out that this is an official document, with legal standing. The words used have to be the correct legal ones so that the document is valid.

- Explore the meanings of the words. Ask: *What informal words would Alexa be likely to use instead of 'imminent' or 'permanent asylum'?* ('soon' and 'stay here for ever')

- Give out photocopiable page 23 'Formal or informal?' Suggest that Mrs Sanders will speak or write to parents far more formally than Alexa will express herself to her friends and family. Explain that you want Mrs Sanders' more formal language to be translated into Alexa's informal words.

Differentiation
Support: Suggest the children work with a partner and use a dictionary for meanings.

Extension: Ask the children to add four 'translated' examples of their own.

5. Correct terms

Objective
To use grammatical terminology correctly.

What you need
Copies of *The Boy at the Back of the Class*, photocopiable page 24 'Correct terms'.

What to do
- Use this activity after finishing the book.

- Write 'grammatical terminology' on the board. Define 'terminology' as the proper use of terms and correct names. Suggest that grammatical terminology becomes familiar when used regularly.

- Comment on the author's precise use of punctuation. Write these terms on the board: exclamation mark, full stop, apostrophe, comma, inverted commas. Direct the children to the first paragraph of Chapter 26 for Share answers and agree that these terms are familiar. Suggest that some grammatical terminology is used more rarely.

- Write these sentences on the board, highlighting the words or punctuation marks in bold:
  - Reporters were waiting at the school – and this came as a shock.
  - **They** crowded around the children.
  - The children **could** be injured!
  - Luckily, Mrs Saunders reacted**…**

- Give out photocopiable page 24, 'Correct terms'. Pronounce and explain the glossary terms. Ask the children to match the highlighted words or marks in the sentences on the board to the terms.

- Explain that writers have written to the author with their problems. The answers need a term from the glossary and a quoted example from Chapter 17.

Differentiation
Support: Let children work in pairs and discuss their answers.

Extension: Ask children to write example sentences for the glossary terminology.

6. Special endings

Objective
To understand that different endings can spell the same sound ('tial' and 'cial').

What you need
Copies of *The Boy at the Back of the Class*.

What to do
- Complete this activity after finishing the book.

- Suggest that this book often uses the word 'special'. Refer the children to two examples: the storyteller's description of Sundays as 'special Adventure Days' in Chapter 5; Ms Duncan's presentation of an envelope with 'special news' in Chapter 26.

- Write the word 'special' on the board. Remind the children that words rhyme if they end with the same sound. Suggest 'partial', but do not write it. Ask the children to write it on individual whiteboards.

- Let the children hold up their spellings and compare results. Ask: *Is it surprising if the incorrect 'parcial' spelling mistake is made?* (no) *Why?* (The final sound is identical in 'special'.) Write the correct spelling, 'partial', on the board.

- Explain that 'cial' and 'tial' endings are easily confused, but that there are spelling rules:
  - If the ending follows a vowel letter, the ending is usually 'cial (for example 'special').
  - If the ending follows a consonant letter, the ending is usually 'tial' for example 'partial')

- Ask the children to complete these words with the correct endings by following the spelling rules: residen…, confiden…, presiden…, fa…, so…, offi…, essen…, artifi…..

- Put the children into pairs to check results and to discuss meanings. Share results as a class.

Differentiation
Support: Suggest children circle the final letter before adding an ending.

Extension: Ask children to write sentences using the words.

Degrees of possibility

- Sort these adverbs into the two boxes below.

certainly possibly obviously definitely perhaps maybe clearly probably

Adverbs that indicate that something will happen	Adverbs that indicate less certainty about something

- Use the adverbs to fill the gaps in the following sentences.

Ahmet was _____ lonely.

He _____ wanted a friend.

_____, no one spoke his language.

_____, the storyteller wanted to be his friend.

_____ he liked lemon sherbets.

It was _____ worth a try.

- Modal verbs can help to make meaning clear. Decide where each modal verb best belongs and write it in the chart.

must ought may can will should shall might would could

Possibility	Certainty	Duty	Ability

Formal or informal?

- Mrs Sanders writes formally to the parents while Alexa speaks informally to her friends. Make sure the message is the same. The first one has been done for you.

Mrs Sanders' formal words and phrases	Alexa's informal words and phrases
An unfortunate incident occurred in the outdoor play area.	Something terrible happened in the playground.
Newspaper reporters gained entry to the premises.	
An unseemly scuffle occurred.	
I cannot be certain how the crowd was allowed to assemble.	
Available staff gained control of the situation.	
The crowd was dispersed and the premises were cleared of reporters.	
No child sustained an injury.	
Henceforth, ball games will be prohibited.	
Additional staff will be positioned at the gates.	

Correct terms

Glossary

modal verb: a verb that helps another verb by changing its meaning (such as 'can' or 'must')

personal pronoun: a word standing in place of a name

ellipsis: three dots that indicate that indicate that more information will follow

dash: a punctuation mark that may be used alone or in pairs to separate some information from the main sentence

- Complete the author's answers to the problems sent to her. Use a term from the glossary and an example from Chapter 17 of the text.

1. Problem: I seem to keep repeating my character's name.

Solution: Think about using a

_____.

My example: _____

_____.

3. Problem: How can I make my verb into the future tense?

Solution: You need to add a

_____.

My example: _____

_____.

2. Problem: I have some extra information to add to the main sentence.

Solution: Join it on with a

_____.

My example: _____

_____.

4. Problem: I want to show that more information will follow.

Solution: Put an

_____.

My example: _____

_____.

PLOT, CHARACTER AND SETTING ▶

1. Laying clues

Objective
To predict what might happen from details stated and implied.

What you need
Copies of *The Boy at the Back of the Class*, photocopiable page 29 'Laying clues'.

What to do
- Use this activity after reading Chapter 1.

- Read the chapter's opening sentence aloud. Ask: *What does 'my' reveal?* (The story is written in the first person.) Suggest that this style of writing puts considerable focus on the storyteller. *Why?* (Events are related from that point of view.)

- Examine what we learn about the storyteller in this chapter. Encourage partner discussion before you progress to class discussion. Prompt by asking: *Is the storyteller sociable? What is liked and disliked? What is their attitude to school?* Point out references to adventure, Tintin comics and 'three best friends'.

- Return to the chapter's opening sentence and make the link between the chapter title and 'empty chair'. Ask: *Is the phrase also a connection with the book's title? Does this suggest that Ahmet is the main character?* Share opinions.

- Comment that you have read only Chapter 1. This is a long book with much to happen yet. Suggest that it would be useful to record what they notice, think and predict at different stages. Give out photocopiable page 29 'Laying clues' for the children to complete.

Differentiation
Support: Let partners prepare together, but encourage a personal reaction to the story.

Extension: Encourage longer entries, individual thinking and references to the text to justify answers.

2. Creating adventures

Objective
To identify how language, structure and presentation contribute to meaning.

What you need
Copies of *The Boy at the Back of the Class*.

What to do
- After reading Chapter 8, comment on its title. Ask: *Is this an adventure?* Remind the children of 'Extra-Special Adventure' and 'excited' in Chapter 1. Ask: *Does the storyteller view ordinary occasions as adventures?*

- Together, scan Chapter 8's early part. Point out how the storyteller chooses when to ask, 'Mum, where's Syria?'; the accumulation of knowledge from an atlas and Aunty Selma's cooking; and the growing enthusiasm. Ask: *Who suggests finding a pomegranate? Who first says 'adventure'?* (Mum) Together, make notes on these stages, before the children write a short paragraph about how the idea of the shopping trip is developed.

- Scan the first half of the trip. Ask: *How is time emphasised?* ('looking at her watch', 'walked for five minutes') Point out changes between walking and using a bus, and the words 'felt like an awfully long way away' to show distance. Ask: *What does Mum say that heightens the drama?* ('the next stop will have to be our last one') Let the children write a second paragraph about this part and how atmosphere and excitement are created.

- Explore the descriptions of market stalls, smells, sights and noise. Discuss the final shop and the owner's appearance and manner. Ask: *Does he improve the adventure?* Let the children write a third paragraph about the progress of the adventure and the writing devices used.

Differentiation
Support: Accept less writing with greater reliance on discussion.

Extension: Expect greater insight.

PLOT, CHARACTER AND SETTING

3. Understanding more

Objective
To make comparisons within and across books.

What you need
Copies of *The Boy at the Back of the Class*, photocopiable page 29 'Laying clues'.

Cross-curricular link
PSHE

What to do
- Complete this activity after reading Chapter 12.

- Ask partners to scan Chapter 12. Ask: *What does the storyteller learn about Ahmet's family now? Where is his father? What has happened to his sister?* Point out detail about his parents ('Maybe he in France' and 'Mum sick' when he points to a picture of a tent).

- Ask: *What does Ahmet do when the storyteller asks 'Syrah…she is…in the sea?'* (He 'nodded and rubbed his eyes'.) Discuss the storyteller's question and Ahmet's reaction. Ask: *Is the storyteller too inquisitive? What evidence suggests that the storyteller understands Ahmet's feelings?* Point out the preceding paragraphs and the storyteller's thoughts about grief.

- Comment that Ahmet only reveals these details to the storyteller. Ask: *Is this surprising? Why does he not tell Josie and Michael when they arrive?* Suggest that he could have formed a closer bond with the storyteller.

- Read the final two paragraphs of Chapter 12 aloud. Consider the storyteller's sympathetic understanding and the silent promise to keep Ahmet's secrets. Ask: *What surprising admission does the storyteller make?* (The promise will be broken the next day.) *What could the 'Something' be?*

- Give out photocopiable page 29 'Laying clues' for the children to complete. Bring the class together to discuss how their views have changed from the first time they completed this sheet (Activity 1).

Differentiation
Support: Remind children to record personal opinions.

Extension: Encourage longer entries and independent thinking.

4. Special friends

Objective
To infer characters' feelings and motives from their actions in a book.

What you need
Copies of *The Boy at the Back of the Class*, photocopiable page 30 'Special friends'.

Cross-curricular link
PSHE

What to do
- Complete this activity after reading Chapter 14.

- Suggest that the storyteller, Josie, Michael and Tom have a particularly close friendship. Ask: *How is this shown in Chapter 14?* Guide the children in scanning the chapter. Point out willingness to listen to one another's plans and the respect they show one another. Ask: *Who does not have a plan?* (the storyteller) *How do the others react?* (They accept it.)

- Look back at Chapter 6 together. Point out the children's generosity with their gifts. Ask: *How do they show friendliness in Chapter 7?* (They invite the new boy to play football.) Comment on their protectiveness and courage as they try to defend him from Brendan and Mr Irons.

- Suggest that as well as being similar, the four children are also different. Look at Chapter 1 and ask: *Who finds maths hard?* (the storyteller) *Who is clumsy?* (Michael)

- Give out individual copies of photocopiable page 30 'Special friends'. In the top half, they should identify shared characteristics; in the bottom half, they should write adjectives that apply to individual children. Encourage them to scan the chapters to find evidence.

Differentiation
Support: Reduce the choice, leaving only the most appropriate adjectives.

Extension: Ask children to write a sketch of a character, using the chosen adjectives.

5. Effective language

Objective

To discuss and evaluate how authors use language, including figurative language, considering the impact on the reader.

What you need

Copies of *The Boy at the Back of the Class*.

What to do

- After reading Chapter 24, comment on the author's powerful descriptions, many linked to the story's 'adventures'.

- Direct the children to Chapter 1's second paragraph and read it aloud. Suggest the children exchange partner responses before you accept answers from individuals. Ask: *How does the author involve you in the storyteller's excitement? Which words do you find effective?* Comment on the repetition of 'new'; powerful words ('hunt', 'excited', 'jumpy', 'whole', 'huge'); travelling away from a place with only 'nice' and 'boring' stationery.

- Move to Chapter 8 and the market. Read aloud the paragraph beginning 'The next place…'. Ask: *Which senses are awakened? Which words paint the most vivid pictures for you? Why?* Point out the alliterative 'Peter never picked potatoes' and the powerful verb 'scrunched'.

- Move to the London adventure in Chapter 19. Read the last two paragraphs aloud. Ask: *What noises, sights and sensations are described? Which words affect you most?* Point out the simile in the final sentence: 'like a big plate of runny jelly'.

- Ask the children to write three short paragraphs describing their reactions to these three descriptions and quoting from the text.

Differentiation

Support: Encourage partner discussion but independent writing.

Extension: Ask children to write about their reactions to Chapter 24's paragraph describing the interview (beginning 'It only lasted ten minutes…').

6. Confusing dialogue

Objective

To identify how language, structure and presentation contribute to meaning.

What you need

Copies of *The Boy at the Back of the Class*.

Cross-curricular link

PSHE

What to do

- Use this activity after finishing the book. When posing questions, encourage partner discussion before accepting individual answers.

- Comment that dialogue has considerable effect on the plot. Point out Chapter 4, when the four friends wait for Ahmet to come out of school. Investigate the adults' conversation. Ask: *What is the conversation about?* (A refugee child has joined the school.) *How does Mrs Grimsby feel?* (His arrival will be a problem.) *What is Mr Brown's reaction?* (He is sympathetic to people trying to escape war.)

- Ask the children to divide their page into four columns with these headings: 'Who is talking'; 'What is talked about'; 'Which important words are used'; 'Who listens and becomes confused'. Ask the children to write in the columns about this conversation.

- Direct the children to the beginning of Chapter 6 and investigate the friends' dialogue at the bus stop. Ask: *What is it about? Who becomes confused? Why?* Invite the children to write about this conversation in the four columns.

- Ask the children to explore and write about the bus conversation heard by the storyteller in Chapter 13, and Mrs Sanders' explanation about the Queen's powers in Chapter 22.

Differentiation

Support: Use partner discussion as a preparation for writing.

Extension: Ask children to identify and write about other dialogue.

7. Reality and story

Objective
To identify and discuss themes in a wide range of writing.

What you need
Copies of *The Boy at the Back of the Class*, photocopiable page 31 'Reality and story'.

Cross-curricular links
History, geography

What to do
- After finishing *The Boy at the Back of the Class*, suggest that the story has a serious theme. Ask: *What is it?* (A refugee's family needs asylum.) Share memories of the book and point out the reference to refugees in Chapter 4; Mum's explanation in Chapter 5; Ms Hemsi's information about Syria in Chapter 6; and, most importantly, Ahmet's own stories in Chapters 10 and 12.

- Investigate the final chapter. Ask: *Who is Ms Duncan? Is her explanation about the Home Office realistic?* Examine the document Alexa and Mum read aloud. Ask: *Where was Ahmet's father found?* (Calais Refugee Camp)

- Revise and note brief references to Ahmet's journey: he is good at climbing and running because of climbing fences; when bullied in the camp his father told him to fight.

- Give out photocopiable page 31 'Reality and story' and go through the information together. Explain that the children must match each section with part of the story that relates to it, giving the chapter number and describing, or quoting, what happens or is said. Partner work may be helpful.

Differentiation
Support: Encourage partner work, with discussion before writing. Help to identify relevant chapters.

Extension: Expect more quoting and closer reference to the text.

8. Influential adults

Objective
To provide reasoned justification for their views.

What you need
Copies of *The Boy at the Back of the Class*.

Cross-curricular link
PSHE

What to do
- Complete this activity after finishing the book. Point out that children are very much the main characters in this book, but adults have important roles.

- When posing the questions suggested here, encourage partner discussion before progressing to whole-class exchanges and references to the text. Ask: *Which four adult characters do you think are important? Why?* Point out that there are no correct answers: it is a matter of opinion.

- Investigate some adults. Pick out Ms Hemsi's role as Ahmet's translator. Ask: *How does Mrs Khan affect the storyteller and Ahmet? Is it important that Mrs Sanders acts decisively against Brendan and Mr Irons? Does Stan's kindness affect the plot?*

- Consider Mum's role in the story. Ask: *How does she show strong feelings about prejudice against refugees? How does she set a good example to others?* (She rises above Frank's rudeness in Chapter 8.) *What is Mum's clever contribution to success for Ahmet and his family?* (Doing the interview reveals the truth.)

- Ask the children to divide a page into four sections. In each section, they should name an adult character that they think influences the plot and provide reasons and evidence. Finally, they must choose the adult that they think matters most.

Differentiation
Support: Expect less writing and support children with suggestions of where to find evidence.

Extension: Look for perceptive comments and independent thinking.

Laying clues

Complete the sheet below with your thoughts and predictions about the story so far.

Date:	Chapter finished:
What I know about the storyteller	What I know about Ahmet

I think the main character will be _____

These are the clues that make me think that:

Another important piece of information or important character may be:

My reaction to the story so far:

I think this will happen next:

Special friends

- How are the storyteller, Michael, Josie and Tom similar?
  Which four adjectives describe them all? Provide some evidence from the story.

Adjectives
sporty   clumsy   kind   inquisitive   thoughtful   imaginative
friendly   brave   clever   awkward   careless   confused
curious   generous   amusing   loyal   reassuring   clever   quiet
adventurous   respectful   patient   protective   funny   anxious

Adjective: _____

Evidence:

Adjective: _____

Evidence:

Adjective: _____

Evidence:

Adjective: _____

Evidence:

- How are the children different? Write two adjectives for each. Choose from the box or write your own.

Michael is _____ and _____.

Evidence: _____

_____

Josie is _____ and _____.

Evidence: _____

_____

Tom is _____ and _____.

Evidence: _____

_____

Reality and story

- Match each piece of reality to where it is referred to in the fictional story. Provide the chapter number, describe what is happening, and quote some words.

Reality

Story

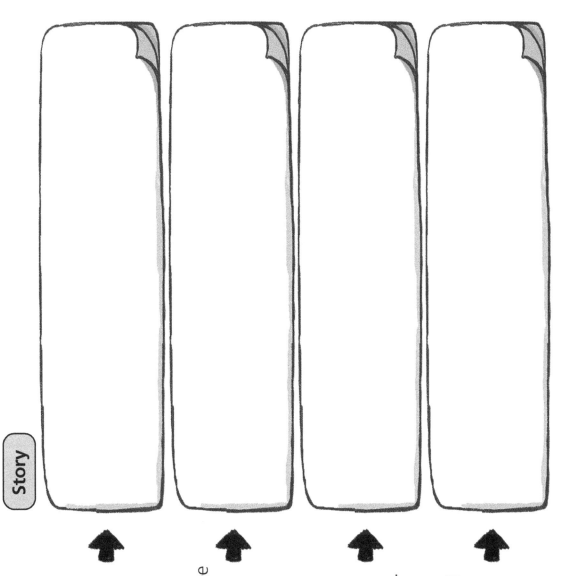

1. The Syrian civil war has been going on since 2011. Syrian people have suffered bombing and the destruction of their homes.

2. The war in Syria has caused a major refugee crisis. Millions of Syrians have fled their country to seek asylum elsewhere. Some Syrians want to reach Europe.

3. Many asylum seekers have been kept in large camps in Europe, such as the overcrowded one in Calais, France. Some want to travel to England and seek asylum.

4. Gaining asylum can be difficult. Status and background must be confirmed before the Home Office makes a decision on an application to stay in the UK.

TALK ABOUT IT ▶

1. Off to London!

Objective
To participate in discussions, role play and improvisations.

What you need
Copies of *The Boy at the Back of the Class*.

Cross-curricular link
PSHE

What to do

- After reading Chapter 17, suggest that going to London sounds more exciting than staying at school. Comment that less sensible friends would find it hard to agree who went.

- Ask: *Which one person most deserves to go to London? Why?* (It is the storyteller's plan.)

- Set the scenario: the friends agree that the storyteller will travel to London with one friend. The two people must work well together, so the storyteller must choose who goes.

- Put the children in pairs. Explain that the storyteller is first going to talk to Michael and check his suitability. Ask partners to have an improvised conversation, one of them acting as the storyteller and one of them as Michael. After two minutes, stop the conversations, leaving one pair in role for the others to listen to. Question and judge how well they get on.

- Hold similar paired conversation between the storyteller and Josie, and the storyteller and Tom. Encourage partners to change roles so that each has a turn as the storyteller. For each conversation, stop with one pair in role so that the class overhear their conversation and question them.

- Afterwards, ask: *Who seems to be the best match to join the storyteller? Why? Does the author agree?*

Differentiation
Support: Provide children with dialogue openers.

Extension: Expect understanding of the friends' strengths and weaknesses.

2. What a day!

Objective
To give well-structured narratives for different purposes, including for expressing feelings.

What you need
Copies of *The Boy at the Back of the Class*, photocopiable page 35 'What a day!'.

Cross-curricular link
Drama

What to do

- After reading Chapter 20, comment that the author has devoted three chapters to the day in London. Ask: *What does this suggest?* (The day is important to the story.)

- Guide the children in scanning Chapters 18, 19 and 20, but focus on the storyteller and Tom. Ask: *Are their experiences and emotions identical?* Point out 'Now that I wasn't feeling so nervous' in Chapter 18 and Tom's earlier 'Come on' and 'Go on'. Ask: *Is Tom less nervous than the storyteller?* Remind the children that at the end of Chapter 19, the storyteller loses consciousness.

- Comment that after so much drama, Tom and the storyteller must long to tell their story.

- Give out photocopiable page 35 'What a day!' for the children to complete. In role, as the storyteller or Tom, they will tell, not read, their story, so this sheet of cue cards needs brief notes and sketches to remind them of events.

- Having completed the page of cue cards, let partners practise their storytelling on each other before progressing to speaking to a group. Remind them that voice, eye contact and body language are all relevant, particularly when expressing feelings.

Differentiation
Support: Encourage pictorial cues and one-word notes in a reduced number of cards.

Extension: Ask children to take the role of a Coldstream Guard to narrate the events.

3. Thinking twice

Objective
To consider and evaluate different viewpoints.

What you need
Copies of *The Boy at the Back of the Class*.

Cross-curricular link
PSHE

What to do

- After finishing Chapter 22, suggest that Josie has conflicting loyalties: her parents and their views about refugee children versus her friends and Ahmet.

- Direct the children to Chapter 6's second paragraph and the conflict between Josie's father's views and instructions and what her friends say. Ask: *How is Josie left feeling?* ('confused', 'frowning') Identify 'My parents don't like me being friends with Ahmet' in Chapter 17.

- Point out that in Chapter 22 Josie describes lying to Mrs Khan about the storyteller's absence. Ask: *How does Josie feel about this?* Direct the children to the friends' conversation on the bus afterwards ('I feel bad for lying to her').

- Divide the class into two groups: group A represents Josie's loyalty to her friends; group B represents obeying her parents. Group A must think of comments to persuade Josie to lie to Mrs Khan; Group B's comments must stop her.

- Put the two groups into lines facing each other. As Josie, walk down the 'alley' between the lines. As you pass children, nod to them to say their comments. At the end of the alley, make your decision.

- Invite children to play Josie's part, and repeat the activity. Does Josie always reach the same decision?

Differentiation
Support: Let partners prepare comments together.

Extension: Let children create a decision alley for the storyteller deciding whether to break Ahmet's secret in Chapter 13.

4. Responsible adults

Objectives
To articulate and justify answers, arguments and opinions; to infer characters' thoughts and motives.

What you need
Copies of *The Boy at the Back of the Class*, photocopiable page 36 'Responsible adults'.

Cross-curricular link
PSHE

What to do

- After reading Chapter 22, remind the children that Josie and Michael go to school while their two friends travel into London. Ask: *What excuses do they make for the storyteller and Tom's absence? Does Mrs Khan believe them?* (Mrs Khan seems 'upset', so maybe not.) *Should Mrs Khan investigate further?* Share opinions.

- Comment that the storyteller's adventure could easily have led to an accident. Remind the children that the storyteller and Tom encounter adults early in the trip who could question them. Ask: *What effect could adult action have?* (It could remove Tom and the storyteller from danger.)

- Remind the children about the adults whom the storyteller and Tom have contact with on their journey in Chapter 18 (the bus driver; the lady who helps them buy their Tube tickets; the taxi driver). Put the children into pairs to find these people and situations in Chapter 18. Encourage partner discussion: what the adult does, and why; what a responsible adult might be expected to do, and why; and what could then have happened.

- Give out photocopiable page 36 'Responsible adults' and ask the children to write their opinions before holding a group discussion.

Differentiation
Support: Encourage more oral work and sharing of ideas before they write.

Extension: Ask children to add Mrs Khan to the adult list, using information from Chapter 22.

5. Providing answers

> ## Objective
> To ask relevant questions to extend their understanding and knowledge.
>
> ## What you need
> Copies of *The Boy at the Back of the Class*.
>
> ## Cross-curricular link
> PSHE

What to do

- After reading Chapter 23, comment on Mr Irons' role, pointing out that he is on playground duty, yet takes no action over Brendan's song. Suggest that his behaviour is always puzzling and together look back at the other chapters that feature him (Chapter 7, where Mr Irons seems to favour Brendan the bully and ignore the obvious nervousness of a new boy; Chapter 22 where the friends reach the school and he does not protect them from the crowd).

- Set the scenario: Mrs Sanders, although satisfied with Mr Irons' teaching ability and the good progress of his students, is worried by these incidents. She writes to the school governors requesting that Mr Irons is asked to leave the school.

- Suggest that the governors must question Mrs Sanders about her reasons. Ask the children to write two questions they, as governors, would like to ask her.

- Create small groups, with one child in each group taking the hot-seat as Mrs Sanders, the others being the school governors, each asking her one question. Repeat the activity with a different child in the hot-seat before a group discussion on what they, as governors, have found out and considered.

- Afterwards, share findings as a class before they, as school governors, vote on whether to keep Mr Irons.

> ## Differentiation
> **Support:** Provide the children with question openers.
>
> **Extension:** Expect probing questions and convincing role play.

6. Finding a voice

> ## Objective
> To select and use appropriate registers for effective communication.
>
> ## What you need
> Copies of *The Boy at the Back of the Class*, photocopiable page 37 'Finding a voice'.
>
> ## Cross-curricular link
> Drama

What to do

- After reading Chapter 24, ask: *What is Mum's plan? Why does she feel strongly that the children should be interviewed?* Agree that she wants the truth to be told.

- Suggest that the school governors may worry about bad publicity for the school because of newspaper reports. Ask: *What could the newspaper reports have said? What could pupils' parents now worry about?* Let partners exchange answers.

- Share ideas as a class, agreeing that parents may be concerned about playtime behaviour; bullying; unauthorised absences; careless supervision of children; poor awareness of what is happening.

- Imagine that the governors arrange for Mrs Saunders, Mrs Khan and Ms Hemsi to be interviewed by journalists. Ask: *What do the governors hope to present?* (a true picture of the school)

- Ask the children to think about likely questions and responsible answers before they do improvised interviews, with partners taking turns as the interviewer and an interviewee.

- Give out photocopiable page 37 'Finding a voice'. Suggest that these are questions they put to one interviewee. They must write brief notes on the imagined answers.

- Keep the completed photocopiable pages for a writing task later.

> ## Differentiation
> **Support:** Let children hear good examples of the oral improvised interviews.
>
> **Extension:** Ask children to create another page of notes for a second interview.

 # What a day!

Write notes and make sketches to fill in the cards.

Use them to help you tell the story from the storyteller or Tom's point of view.

Introducing yourself

Who are you?

What were your feelings and actions at the bus stop this morning?

Managing at the Tube station

Did you have any problems? If so, what were they?

Was it easy to know which trains to get on?

The taxi ride

Did you get a taxi easily? What happened?

Was the fare expensive?

Buckingham Palace

Did you hand over the note? If so, how?

Did you talk to the Queen?

Coming home in a police car

What were you worried about?

What were you happy about?

TALK ABOUT IT

Responsible adults

- Write about how these adults behaved and what could have been more responsible action.

The adult	What the adult in the story does and why	What a responsible adult would do and why	What would happen next
The bus driver			
The lady at the Tube			
The taxi driver			

Finding a voice

Person interviewed _____ Age: _____

Position in Nelson School _____

What is your connection with the new boy?

Did you know his background before he came?

Were you worried about him making friends?

Did you know about the plan to go to London?

Were you suspicious when two friends were absent?

Did those children just want a day out?

Is this sort of thing likely to happen again?

Is there truth in the rumours about bullies and uncaring teachers?

Special observations

GET WRITING ▶

1. Working together

What to do

- After reading Chapter 17, discuss what 'writing cohesion' means. Agree that it means that written parts fit together smoothly. Ask: *What are the smaller parts?* (sentences) *What are the larger parts?* (paragraphs)

- Direct the children to the beginning of Chapter 13. Ask them to scan, independently or with a partner, the first five paragraphs and write down three phrases that link a paragraph to the preceding writing. Share the findings: 'The night after', 'By the time', 'That morning' and 'At first'. Point out that these phrases bring cohesion by confirming the sequence of events.

- Read the first paragraph of Chapter 13 aloud. Point out 'they' in the third sentence. Ask: *Whom is this pronoun referring to?* (sheep) Explain that pronouns improve cohesion within a paragraph by referring to earlier words. Identify 'he' and 'him' in the second paragraph and 'they' in the fourth paragraph.

- Examine the diagram of the storyteller's Emergency Plan in Chapter 17. Comment on the importance of the storyteller's friends understanding what to do.

- Ask the children to write an explanation of about three paragraphs to accompany this plan. Emphasise the need for cohesion within and across the paragraphs. Suggest writing a rough draft first, editing and copying out their final version.

2. In print

What to do

- After finishing Chapter 24, display photocopiable page 37 'Finding a voice'. Remind the children that they previously completed this interview form, writing the notes that they, as a journalist, made during an imaginary interview with Mrs Sanders, Mrs Khan or Ms Hemsi.

- Give out the children's completed copies of photocopiable page 37 for them to refresh their memories. In small groups, invite them to explain their notes to one another.

- Explain that they, as journalists, must write their newspaper article. Show the children some examples of articles in a local newspaper. Point out common features: an attention-grabbing headline; an introductory paragraph setting the scene and answering the five Ws (What? Where? When? Why? Who?); people's names and ages; third-person writing; connectives; interesting quotations from the people involved; a powerful closing statement.

- Ask the children to write their articles. The newspaper editor has given them an allowance of 250 to 300 words. Suggest using a computer and the word-count facility, and to be willing to edit.

3. Star rating

Objective
To evaluate by assessing the effectiveness of others' writing.

What you need
Copies of *The Boy at the Back of the Class*, photocopiable page 41 'Star rating'.

What to do
- After finishing the book, ask: *What did you think of this novel? Did you enjoy it?* Encourage partner and group exchanges before progressing to class discussion.

- Ask the children to put themselves in your position: a class teacher of the same age group next year. Ask: *Should I choose this book again?* Put the children into small groups to produce two lists: one for choosing the book and one against. Share the points.

- Point out the 2018 publication date. Explain that teachers, children and publishers' magazines and websites may all have contained reviews of the book. Reviewers would have written short pieces about the book, expressing their personal views.

- Show the children the arts review section of a newspaper (such as 'The Sunday Times') where television programmes, shows, films and new books are reviewed. Point out where stars are used to rate work. Suggest that this is a quick way to sum up the reviewer's feelings and the extent of their recommendation.

- Give out photocopiable page 41 'Star rating' for the children to write a review of *The Boy at the Back of the Class*. Ask them to write complete sentences for most sections.

Differentiation
Support: Let partners discuss their answers before writing.

Extension: Invite children to write a review of another book they have read recently.

4. Dear Diary…

Objective
To write in narrative form, by describing settings, characters and atmosphere.

What you need
Copies of *The Boy at the Back of the Class*, photocopiable page 42 'Dear Diary…'.

What to do
- Use this activity after finishing the book.

- Comment that Mum is a very busy, hard-working parent. Ask: *How can you tell she has little money to spare?* (In Chapter 8 she is concerned that two pomegranates will be too expensive and in Chapter 26 she cannot afford goodie bags for a birthday party.)

- Suggest that her life may feel quite lonely as she has few adults to talk to. Uncle Lenny only visits 'sometimes' and her best friend, Aunty Selma, (Chapter 8) now lives in Turkey. Ask: *Does Mum have many friendly neighbours to talk to now?* Point out the hostility from Mr Greggs in Chapter 21, and that it is not until Chapter 26 that Mr and Mrs Rashid show increased friendliness.

- Suggest that it would help Mum to write down her thoughts and concerns sometimes in a diary. Discuss together some key moments when she might write her diary, for example, after Chapter 8, as she reflects on the shopping trip and Frank's attitude; after Chapter 20 as she waits for Alexa to come back from London; and before Chapter 26 when she puts Dad's card out.

- Give out photocopiable page 42 'Dear Diary…' and invite the children to scan the relevant chapters before writing two diary entries by Mum.

Differentiation
Support: Encourage partner discussion when children are deciding what to write.

Extension: Expect more variety in the mood of the diary entries.

5. Alexa's adventures

Objective
To plan their writing by noting and developing initial ideas, drawing on reading.

What you need
Copies of *The Boy at the Back of the Class*, photocopiable page 43 'Alexa's adventures'.

What to do
- After finishing the book, comment that many novels have sequels. Mention the *Harry Potter* series and request examples from the children. Ask: *Is a sequel likely here? What makes you think that?* Let partners, and then the class, share opinions.

- Read the penultimate paragraph of the book aloud. Draw attention to 'and the beginning of a whole set of new adventures'. Suggest that here the author allows herself the opportunity for writing a sequel.

- Create small discussion groups. Ask: *What would you make the sequel about? Where would its main setting be? Who would be the main characters? What would the adventures involve? How could they be linked?*

- Share ideas as a class, prompting with questions: *Will Ahmet stay with the friends or move to another part of the country? Will someone mysterious arrive? Will Brendan be replaced by another bully? Will the next class teacher be less pleasant?*

- Read the book's penultimate sentence aloud again. Suggest that it implies continuing with Alexa as the storyteller, still with a strong interest in adventures.

- Give out photocopiable page 43 'Alexa's adventures' for the children to make notes, planning a sequel to this book. Suggest they make their final planning decisions and draft rough notes before completing the photocopiable page.

Differentiation
Support: Let partners exchange ideas before working independently.

Extension: Expect original ideas.

6. Starting again

Objective
To draft and write by selecting appropriate grammar and vocabulary, understanding how such choices can change and enhance meaning.

What you need
Copies of *The Boy at the Back of the Class*, the children's completed copies of photocopiable page 43 'Alexa's adventures'.

What to do
- Use this activity after finishing the book and doing Activity 5 'Alexa's adventures'.

- Direct the children to 'and the beginning of a whole set of new adventures' in the book's penultimate paragraph and remind them that this prompted their plan of a sequel.

- Investigate the opening paragraphs of *The Boy at the Back of the Class*. Discuss how the author has created a good opening. Pick out: intriguing chapter title; repetition of that phrase in the early paragraphs; the interesting 'voice' of the storyteller; information and description; reference to 'Adventure'. Suggest a reader would want the same style in a sequel's opening.

- Return the children's completed plans from Activity 5. Let them revise their contents by explaining them to a partner before writing their opening pages.

- Put the children into small groups. Ask them to read their opening pages aloud to one another for peer reviews. Encourage positive and helpful feedback, perhaps in a 'sandwich' response: two aspects the listener liked, separated by a helpful suggestion for what the writer needs to think about now.

- Use an extended writing session to complete the opening chapter.

Differentiation
Support: Use partner review for less confident writers.

Extension: Expect children to open their sequel well and to use the author's style.

Star rating

- Use this sheet to help you write a review of *The Boy at the Back of the Class*.

Title: _____   **Author:** _____

About the story:

_____

_____

_____

_____

Special features:

_____

_____

_____

My favourite part: **My least favourite part:**

_____   _____

_____   _____

_____   _____

_____   _____

Who would enjoy this story?:

_____

_____

Star rating: ☆ ☆ ☆ ☆ ☆

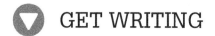

Dear Diary...

- Write Mum's diary at two points in the story.

Chapter:

Dear Diary

_____

_____

_____

_____

_____

_____

_____

_____

Chapter:

Dear Diary

_____

_____

_____

_____

_____

_____

_____

_____

_____

_____

Alexa's adventures

- Write notes planning a sequel to *The Boy at the Back of the Class*.

Possible title

Structure
How the sequel will be divided

How will the book end?

Who?
Who will be the main character(s)?

How old will they be?

What?
What will be the book's main theme?

What will happen at the start?

When?
How much time will have passed since the first book?

What will have changed since then?

Where?
Where will the main setting be?

Will there be other locations?

SEQUEL

ASSESSMENT ▶

1. Ahmet or Alexa?

Objective
To provide reasoned justification for their views.

What you need
Copies of *The Boy at the Back of the Class*, an enlarged copy of photocopiable page 29 'Laying clues'.

What to do
- Use this activity after finishing the text and doing Activity 1, page 25 'Laying clues'. Encourage partner exchanges before class discussion.

- Display an enlarged, unused copy of photocopiable page 29 'Laying clues'. Point out the questions about the main character.

- Remind the children that they first filled in the page after reading Chapter 1 of the book. Invite the children to scan Chapter 1. Ask: *Can you remember who you thought the main character would be? Why?*

- Guide the children in scanning Chapters 2 to 12. Explain that the children completed the photocopiable again at this point. Ask: *Did your view change? Why?*

- Together scan the rest of the book, concentrating on events and remarks that focus on Ahmet or the storyteller.

- Ask the children to divide a page into two, one half entitled 'Ahmet', the other half 'Alexa'. In each half, the children must identify four different events between Chapter 13 and the end of the book, that indicate that this character is the main one and explain the event's importance.

- Finally, they must choose whether Ahmet or Alexa is the book's main character and explain why.

Differentiation
Support: Let partners collaborate on identifying evidence, but write their notes independently.

Extension: Encourage children to write a few paragraphs explaining their choice.

2. Placing books

Objective
To explain and discuss their understanding of what they have read.

What you need
Copies of *The Boy at the Back of the Class*.

What to do
- Use this activity after finishing the book.

- Ask the children to imagine being a bookshop owner placing this book in a category in the shop. They need to answer these questions: *Is it for adults or children? Is it fiction or non-fiction?* (children's fiction).

- Divide the children into pairs. Ask them to discuss their experiences of looking for a fiction book in a bookshop or library. Pose questions: *How do you start? Do you look for a favourite author? An interesting cover or title?* Share class experiences.

- Explain that many shops divide children's fiction into story types. Ask: *What categories would you expect?* List common sections on the board: 'Fantasy', 'Animal stories', 'School stories', 'Adventure', 'Serious issues'.

- Ask the children, first in pairs, and then doubled into larger groups, to discuss where they would place this book and why. Finally, ask everyone to write down their individual decision and, in a few lines, to explain why.

- Share the results. Is the book in 'Adventure' because of the storyteller's interest in this subject? Is it in 'Serious issues' because the book is about a real war and problems faced by asylum seekers?

Differentiation
Support: Explain the section titles and suggest ways to decide. Emphasise that there is no correct answer.

Extension: Ask children to describe and place a book they have read recently.

3. According to Stan

Objective
To write a narrative, describing settings, characters and atmosphere and integrating dialogue to convey character and advance the action.

What you need
Copies of *The Boy at the Back of the Class*.

What to do

- After finishing the book, comment on the first-person writing. Ask: *Do you like this style? Are there advantages and disadvantages?* Let partners exchange opinions before class discussion. Suggest that the reader may feel more drawn into the story because the storyteller is directly involved in the action. However, there may be points in the story when the reader would be interested in learning about events from a different character's point of view.

- Remind the children about the London taxi ride. Suggest partners scan the final pages of Chapter 18. Ask: *How do the children meet Stan? Does he offer them a ride immediately? What sort of person does he seem?*

- Point out Stan's early actions: 'looked around'; questioned them being on their own; 'frowning'. Ask: *What do the actions suggest? Is he worried?*

- Ask the children to rewrite this part of the chapter (where Stan picks them up and takes them to Buckingham Palace) with Stan as the storyteller. He will recount the trip as he remembers it and describe what he thought. Words, details and dialogue will not be the same, but the writing will still be in the first person.

Differentiation
Support: Re-read the taxi-ride passage together and provide a sentence opener.

Extension: Encourage children to reveal more of Stan's personality and opinions. They could also include his interview on television (Chapter 21).

4. A moral conscience

Objective
To infer characters' feelings, thoughts and motives from their actions, and to justify inferences with evidence.

What you need
Copies of *The Boy at the Back of the Class*.

Cross-curricular link
PSHE

What to do

- After finishing the book, focus on Mum. Encourage partner exchanges before accepting answers to these questions: *Is Mum strong or weak? Is she important? Does she influence others?*

- Remind the children that Mum is a hard-working single parent, who turns shopping trips into exciting adventures. Suggest that she is also the book's moral conscience, with strong views about right and wrong.

- Identify four occasions when something is said or done that reveals Mum's moral convictions (Alexa says 'refugee kid' in Chapter 5; Mum encounters Frank, the floor manager, in Chapter 8; Mr Greggs comes to the door in Chapter 21; the newspaper quotes Mr Fry in Chapter 24). List these incidents on the board.

- Re-read Mum and Frank's dialogue in Chapter 8. Ask: *What does Frank do wrong?* (He pays little attention to Mum.) *How does Mum respond? Why?* (She is 'nice to him' in order to rise above his unpleasant behaviour, not stoop to his low level.)

- Draw a chart on the board that has three columns with these headings: 'An unpleasant action or word'; 'How Mum responds'; 'Mum's intention'.

- Working on one incident at a time, the children should write one or two sentences in each column.

Differentiation
Support: Encourage preliminary partner discussion. If needed, assess children orally.

Extension: Ask children to develop their sentences into paragraphs about Mum's character.

5. Chapter 27

Objective
To note and develop initial ideas, drawing on reading and research where necessary.

What you need
Copies of *The Boy at the Back of the Class*, photocopiable page 47 'Chapter 27'.

What to do
- Use this activity after finishing the book. When posing questions, encourage partner exchanges before progressing to whole-class discussion.

- Point out that a function of the book's ending is to tie up loose ends in the plot. Remind the children of the Queen's invitation in Chapter 25. Suggest that a chapter about this trip to Buckingham Palace would make an exciting end and an opportunity for adventure.

- Explain that you want the children to plan a short Chapter 27. (The present text ends with Chapter 26.) Chapter 27 must be about their adventurous trip, with different people and vehicles, to Buckingham Palace.

- Encourage partners and then the class to share ideas. Suggest that the friends travel without adults. Ask: *Do they leave something on the Tube train? Do they get off at the wrong station? Do they run short of time? Does Stan help out with his taxi? Do they catch a bus? Does one person get separated from the others?* Listen to suggestions and note some on the board.

- Give out photocopiable page 47 'Chapter 27'. Suggest the children use the same pictorial style as the plan in Chapter 15, but with notes included. Retain children's completed sheets for the next activity.

Differentiation
Support: Encourage further paired discussion after children have made their pictorial plan and before they write their notes.

Extension: Expect original ideas and clearer notes.

6. Sounding right

Objective
To select the appropriate form and use other similar writing as models for their own.

What you need
Copies of *The Boy at the Back of the Class*, the children's completed photocopiable page 47 'Chapter 27'.

What to do
- Use this activity after finishing the book and completing Assessment Activity 5. Remind the children of the task to plan Chapter 27, in which the friends go to meet the Queen.

- Examine the contents pages at the beginning of the book and point out the varied chapter length. Comment that Chapter 27 will only be about this London adventure, so it can be quite a short chapter. Point out also that the chapters are named as well as numbered.

- Direct the children to Chapter 17 to explore the author's writing style and explore typical writing features. Ask: *Is the chapter title appropriate? How is the text divided? Is there cohesion between and within paragraphs? Is the writing in the first or third person? Is dialogue realistic? Does the author's language distinguish between dialogue and description? Are images vivid?*

- Give out the children's completed photocopiable page 47 'Chapter 27'. Ask them to familiarise themselves with their plan before they start writing. Set aside some extended writing sessions to complete their chapter.

Differentiation
Support: Encourage partners to help each other to go through their plan. Children could write just a section of their chapter.

Extension: Expect the children to find more ways to use the author's style and to write an exciting chapter.

Chapter 27

- Plan Chapter 27, an adventurous trip to Buckingham Palace.

Mum saw us off.

SCHOLASTIC

READ & RESPOND

Available in this series:

978-1407-15879-2

978-1407-14224-1

978-1407-16063-4

978-1407-16056-6

978-1407-14228-9

978-1407-16069-6

978-1407-16070-2

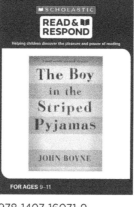

978-1407-16071-9

978-1407-14230-2

978-1407-16057-3

978-1407-16064-1

978-1407-14223-4

978-0702-30890-1

978-0702-30859-8

To find out more,
visit www.scholastic.co.uk/read-and-respond